I love trees best in spring, when coiled buds
    Thrust spears towards the sun; or in the fall,
When mottled leaves lie drowned in autumn floods;
    Or during drowsy summer's blowsy sprawl;
Or dozing boughs, snow laden and at rest.
At all times, you might say—I love trees best!

What Readers and Critics say about the Poetry of Felix Dennis

'Felix Dennis is the real thing. I love reading his verse and you will, too.'
— **Stephen Fry**, *actor, writer, director*

'His poetry sings like a summer breeze through the fairground.'
— **Sir Paul McCartney**, *musician, songwriter*

'A fantastic collection! Rich, sumptuous and beautifully threaded.'
— **Jon Snow**, *television newscaster*

'If Waugh were alive, he would fall on Dennis's verse with a glad cry of recognition and approval.'
— **John Walsh**, *The Independent*

'An engaging monster, filled with contradictions and reeking of sulphur.'
— *The Times*

'I enjoy his poetry immensely.'
— **Mick Jagger**, *singer, songwriter*

'The uncrowned Poet Laureate… he writes in the language of the soul.'
— **Christopher Rush**, *author*

'He invokes sorrow as fast as regret, pain as readily as passion, and love as tenderly as murderous rage.'
— **Shirley Conran**, *author*

'Brilliant, grave, poignant, moving and elemental, Felix Dennis's poetry is music written for the human voice.'
— **V. Sundaram**, *columnist, critic*

'Marvellous stuff… a 21st century Kipling.'
— **Tom Wolfe**, *critic, author*

'The most satisfying collection of poetry I have ever read.'
— **Tracy Farnsworth**, *editor roundtablereviews.com*

'Beautifully crafted and unforgettable. To watch him perform is pure magic.'
— **Clare Fitzsimmons**, *Stratford Observer*

'At least one of these poems will be instantly anthologised.'
— **Melvyn Bragg**, *broadcaster, author*

'Total, utter joy… so real, so readable and so enjoyable.'
— **Richard Fair**, *bbc.co.uk*

'Talent at once wise and maddeningly childish, optimistic and grim.'
— **Dawn French**, *actor, comedienne*

'You feel he lived it so richly, so dangerously, so that he could be so wise for our delight.'
— **Dr. Robert Woof**, *Director of The Wordsworth Trust*

'He makes it look easy, damn him! I couldn't put the book down.'
— **Z. Menthos**, *critic.org*

'His talent leaps off every page.'
— **Alan Caruba**, *editor, bookviews.com*

By the same author

A Glass Half Full
(Hutchinson) 2002

Lone Wolf
(Hutchinson) 2004

The Taking of Saddam:
A Ballad
(Noctua Press) 2004

When Jack Sued Jill:
Nursery Rhymes for Modern Times
(Ebury Press) 2006

Island of Dreams:
99 Poems from Mustique
(Noctua Press) 2007

Homeless in My Heart
(Ebury Press) 2008

All titles are available from good booksellers.

www.felixdennis.com
contains many poems, published and unpublished,
as well as a library of sound recordings and video footage
of Felix Dennis's verse and poetry tours.

TALES FROM THE WOODS

TALES FROM THE WOODS

FELIX DENNIS

With a Foreword by Pauline Buchanan Black

Designed by Rebecca Jezzard · Illustrations by Bill Sanderson

EBURY
PRESS

1 3 5 7 9 10 8 6 4 2

First published in 2010 by Ebury Press, an imprint of Ebury Publishing

A Random House Group Company

The Random House Group Limited Reg. No 954009

Addresses for companies within the Random House Group can be found at
www.randomhouse.co.uk

A CIP catalogue record for this book is available from the British Library.
Also available from the RNIB's National Library Service in Braille, giant print and as a Talking Book.

Illustrator: Bill Sanderson
Designer: Rebecca Jezzard

Printed and bound by Butler, Tanner & Dennis
Frome and London

Set in Sabon and Univers

ISBN: 9780091937676

To buy books by your favourite authors and register for offers visit
www.rbooks.co.uk

FSC
Mixed Sources
Product group from well-managed
forests and other controlled sources
Cert no. SGS-COC-006091
www.fsc.org
©1996 Forest Stewardship Council

For David Bliss,
John Holliday, Stephen Coffey,
Dave Hares, Jeremy Collins, Andy Smith
and so many others who
plant all the trees
while I get all the credit

'*Our Forests are undoubtedly the greatest Magazines of the Wealth and the Glory of this Nation, and our Oaks the truest Oracles of its perpetuity and happiness...*'

— **John Evelyn** *Sylva* (**1664**)

Foreword

By his own admission, Felix Dennis is a tree planter – he plants over 100,000 native broadleaf saplings each year. The man clearly has poetry in his soul, because only someone who sees beauty in trees as a poet does would be inspired to proliferate such beauty for the rest of us to enjoy. That he then makes the emotional investment in writing poetry and putting it before a critical audience, also requires a degree of bravery. To put out a book of poems about trees, therefore, is nothing less than a conjunction of the beautiful and the brave.

These poems are best read under a tree or (if the weather is unkind) at a window with a treescape beyond. That way, you won't have far to look to see what Felix, and The Tree Council, are about. And if it moves you to plant a tree as well, so much the better.

Who is he, though, this poet planter? Can we work that out from the poems in this book? Or read it in his visionary plans to create a large forest in the heart of England? Sometimes, I think he is the embodiment of the Green Man, mysterious, mischievous, peering out of the wild and untamed foliage that surrounds him and springs from him. His aim to connect up a massive network of high forest and large woods with areas of wood pasture and coppice woodland to create a broadleaf ecosystem, marks him out to some as a madman. To others, it's self-evident that this is what the Green Man would want to see. Well, in the end, it doesn't really matter. He will be leaving behind a landscape of the eye and of the soul forever changed by his actions and his words.

— Pauline Buchanan Black
   Director General, The Tree Council

Contents

All Nature's Art

All Nature's Art is purest accident,
Not in or of itself— how should she know?—
But in the quality of what is lent
By those who view what Providence made so.

Take grass of softest green— in beetles' eyes
A dreary, harsh savanna, spiked and bound
In monochrome and perilous disguise:
To us a lawn— to hens, a killing ground.

And so it is, my love, with you and me—
This old fool's eyes were ever drawn to youth;
Though Nature's Art lies not in what we see,
Such 'seeing' smooths the wilderness of truth.

Though as for that, no truth was ever known
To topple skin-deep Beauty from her throne.

An English Light

9:45 on a fine June night,
I watch from the window and write and write
As the fields are lit by the blood-eyed flight
Of the westering sun— as trees ignite,
And the shadows lance in the slanted light,
Each leaf a halo of fire, more bright
Than the pale moon clothed in mottle and white,
Awaiting the arms of her purple knight.

Little is moving in Eden this night:
The ears of an owl on his branchy height,
Or the plop of a frog as he sinks from sight,
As a martin blurs like a sickle kite
Of gunmetal grey… and I write and write
This hymn of delight in an English light.

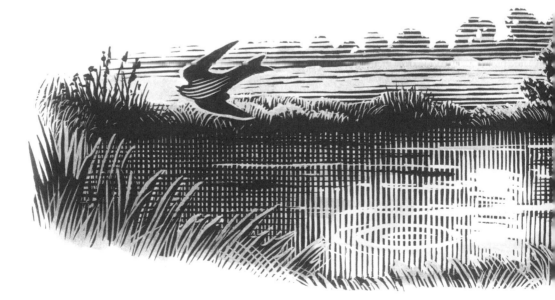

3

An Older England

There has always been in England
  An older England still,
Where Chaucer rode to Canterbury
  And Falstaff drank his fill;

Where poets scrawled immortal lines
  Beside a daffodil,
And lovers lay upon the grass
  Atop of Bredon Hill;

Where parson in his pulpit droned
  As Nancy winked at Bill,
Where Brontës conjured moonlit paths
  And Hardy drowned a mill;

Where jolly tars sailed hearts-of-oak
  From China to Brazil,
And foxes sought out Squire's pack
  To race them for the thrill.

We never could cease worshipping
  What never was— nor will;
There has always been in England
  An older England still.

5

April 15, 2007 7:45 P.M.

A glowing, black-boughed cherry,
In glory on the lawn,
Stands stripped of leaf or berry—
Its wind-whipped blossom borne

As if in mute defiance
Of what I cannot know—
For neither wit nor science
Could match this matchless show—

As now the sun creeps, laden
With orange, twilight fire
To kiss this white-lipped maiden—
And, awe-struck, I retire.

Arrival Of The New Owner

I found two keepers doing their rounds,
  Leading the pheasants from wood to hill,
Their stares as flint as their lurcher hounds:
'And whom be you?' 'I'm walking the bounds
  Of my land,' I said. And stood stock-still.

The elder veteran belched and sighed,
  Snapping commands to his front and back;
With rumbling throats the dogs complied
And slumped to the side of the grassy ride
  As game-birds fluttered across the track.

Then each side spoke — politely enough —
  As I folded my map, shook hands and left;
The skin of their hands was poacher rough,
While the lurchers watched in a wary huff
  And growled to each other of thieves and theft.

And as to that, well, the dogs had cause,
  For though it was true the land was mine,
Paid for, haggled for, clause by clause,
Due stamped and deeded by ancient laws—
  Yet each of us knew, though we gave no sign,

That the land was theirs. And theirs alone.
  That they owned each hanger and stream and hill,
Each wood, each hedge, each meadow and stone—
That I understood what they'd always known:
  The land was theirs. And remained theirs, still.

The meeting is imaginary, but the land is not; nor the truth of what I am trying to say. For six hundred years, the Spernal and Coughton estate was owned by the Throckmorton family of 'Gunpowder Plot' fame. Now a large chunk of those 3,500 acres is mine. It is old land, untroubled by the turmoil of recent centuries for the most part, hoarding its plague pits and marl mines, its ruined nunnery and brooding lakes, its badger sets and ancient bluebell woods to itself. Not to mention some of the finest veteran oaks in England. But it can never be 'mine'. Only those who have lived and worked within its borders (some for generations) can 'own' it. Because they know it as I never can.

As I Spied Swallows Scything...

As I spied swallows scything
  Across an evening sky,
I thought upon those midges
  Whose turn it was to die.

Do midges boast of heroes?
  Are some born lame or halt?
Are geniuses among them
  To reckon blame or fault?

And as they swarm by millions
  In garden, field or fen,
Do midges mourn their fellows?
  Or do they die like men?

Autumn Harvest

Wet leaves littering an unmown lawn;
    Grey clouds scudding from the hills;
Coal-black rooks in the rain-soaked fields;
    Bluebottles dozing on the sills.

Thorn haws glowing in a glittering hedge;
    Fox paws printed in the mud;
Sickle-winged swifts and swallows in the mist,
    Africa singing in their blood.

Drunk brown wasps on a windfall Cox;
    Fat lambs bleating at the ramp;
Shy chanterelles under moss-backed stones;
    Silage spilling from the clamp.

Damp fog silvering a new-ploughed field;
    Urchins drowning in the brooks;
Deep armchairs by an ash-log fire—
    Baccy and bourbon and books!

12

'Urchin' is an old country name for a hedgehog. When hibernating, hedgehogs
sometimes choose daft places to nest. Should such havens be too near a brook
prone to flooding… well, you can guess the rest.

Avon

*Written for the opening ceremony of
the Stratford River Festival, July 2009*

Dear Will,

The silent swans still swim by Clopton Bridge
Though you might blink, amazed at what they see—
Its willow-bordered banks and foliage
Frame views of monuments we raised to *thee*!

From Tewkesbury to Naseby, where she springs,
We call the river *Shakespeare's* Avon now,
And though, by Woollas Hall, a skylark sings,
No horse or oxen strain at any plough,

No rose-lipped maiden strips some rushy mere
Of cuckoo-buds for herbalists or crones;
Still less do young bucks poach proud Lucy's deer
At Charlecote, where the old fool rests his bones.

The Falcon's idle rogues are topers still,
Stout Bidford men can yet out-drink all buyers;
The waters there still wander as they will
And loop their way to Evesham through the Priors.

Wyre Piddle, Welford, Bredon, Grafton, Broom—
Those names you knew have long outlived your clay,
The ghost at Baginton cries out her doom
Though many another haunt has passed away.

So much has changed, so much! and yet the hearts
Of men are as you left them in your prime,
Upon each page, each line— so wise your arts:
'He was not for an age, but for all time!'

And did she stir your dreams or goose-winged pen,
This river, by which worlds extol your name?
Sweet Bard, the words your magic conjured then
Stand dearer to our hearts than all your fame.

Ba-ma-ta

Its bark is scarred— gold lichen clings like hair,
Strange epiphytes and fungi sprout and creep;
The pink-blushed petals scattered round my chair
Tell all who care, this veteran's roots go deep.

Why, such a cedar (*ba-ma-ta* they called it),
Would once have built a ship, so long it's stood—
A whaler, likely. Shipwrights logged and hauled it
Across the seas, so precious was its wood.

The leaves are leather discs; they scud and scrape
Along a shingled roof at night like claws.
Its gnarled old boughs are battered out of shape
From hurricane and blast. Yet still it soars.

For centuries this tree has foiled all powers—
And like old poets— still can conjure flowers.

Growing through the roof of my games room on the Caribbean island of Mustique, its roots far beneath the foundations of the house, a white cedar tree (*Tabebuia heterophylla*) emerges to tower above our sundeck. Gaunt, massive and ancient, it is a great nuisance to our house staff. The blushed-pink and yellow flowers stain flagstones when trodden on. Its detritus blocks gutters. Being deciduous, its leathery leaves have frightened many a guest as they scrape across roofs at night. It has almost no scent and, except for tree-lovers, is not perhaps a thing of beauty, although to me it is because it speaks of the history of the West Indies. In the Carib tongue it was called the 'Ba-ma-ta'. The Caribs used it to build virtually unsinkable boats and canoes with which to colonise the Lesser Antilles. European colonists, in their turn, did much the same. And the flowers really are very beautiful.

Blackthorn Winter

Scraps of blackthorn blossom fleck my coat,
Another gust of hail, and down they float;
A fine spring this— the earth as cold as stone,
North-easterlies that cut you to the bone.

The primroses have withered, one by one,
The bluebells cower, praying for the sun,
Rumbling thunder stalks the streaming hills,
Sneaking frost has slain the daffodils.

My boots are caked in mud; the dog is, too.
Above a clump of ash, the sun breaks through,
A sudden glance of light on bud and bark,
My heart leaps up— the soul song of a lark!

17

The Bluebell Wood

We walked within an ancient wood
Beside the Heart-of-England way
Where oak and beech and hazel stood,
Their leaves the pale shades of May.

By bole and bough, still black with rain,
The sunlight filtered where it would
Across a glowing, radiant stain—
We stood within a bluebell wood!

And stood and stood, both lost for words,
As all around the woodland rang
And echoed with the cries of birds
Who sang and sang and sang and sang…

My mind has marked that afternoon
To hoard against life's stone and sling;
Should I go late, or I go soon,
The bluebells glow— the birds still sing.

The Children Of Wood

Every age is a wood age, as it has been from the first,
A char-fired stick for a weapon— let nature do her worst;
We harried the squealing mammoth to pits of sharpened logs,
Roasting his flesh on wood fires, tossing a bone to our dogs.

From wood we smelted iron— and hollowed the first canoes,
Of wood we built our temples to banish our own taboos,
Wood fired the kilns of our potters, from bark we wove our twine
And fastened the first ship's rigging or fashioned a fishing line.

On wood we rolled our heelstones across a downland moor,
Of wood we built the chariot wheels that filled the world with war,
On wood we first cut tallies, with wood new lines were drawn—
(Beside the walls of Babylon, geometry was born).

Then came a stranger birthing from an exiled eunuch's shame,
T'sai Lun invented paper and the world was never the same,
Paper to paint and scrawl on, paper to still men's fears,
Paper to bridge the lakes of death with the wisdom of our seers.

The keels of our ships were wooden, the pulleys that held our ropes,
The cross of the Christian saviour became the prop of Popes,
And the touch of a joiner's sanding or the love of a craftsman's art
For the hidden grain in a carving, is a thing to lift the heart.

As the logs burn in your fireplace— so the past returns, revealed,
When wood was our only ally, and fire our only shield,
We are wedded to wood as surely as a bole is wedded to bark—
So bless the trees, my children, they kept you from the dark;

They nurtured and they sustained us, they raised us from the dust,
It is time now, to repay them; in truth, we know we must,
Not just for their stately beauty, not just because we should—
We owe them more than duty. We are the children of wood!

City Trees

These trees, which men humiliate,
　Stand patiently in secret joy.
Their brothers wait beyond the gate—
　And where is Carthage?
　　　　Where is Troy?

The Court Of Arden

Oak the King and Beech his Queen,
Willow, the Pretender,
Elm, the Mage who rules unseen,
Ash, a Rake in splendour.

Lime, the bastard half-breed Bard,
Pear, a Duke reclining,
Thorn and Larch the Palace Guard,
Birch, a Princess pining.

Old Sir Yew, rough Lord of Shades,
Begs Prince Hazel's pardon,
Cherry — loveliest of all Maids —
Charms the court of Arden.

Inspired by the wit and affection for trees so clearly evident in
Will Cohu's splendid book, *Out of the Woods* (Short Books, 2007).
The publishers claim it to be 'The Armchair Guide to Trees',
but it's really much better than that. A great read for tree lovers
on a winter evening by the fireside. The colour illustrations by
Mungo McCosh have a strange fascination of their own, too.

Death Of A Pied Wagtail

A blur of grace in brown and grey,
The hawk swooped by my hatless head—
A 'whoosh', a 'whomp', it struck its prey,
Staggered, and made to fly away—
Though as for that, I wished it dead.

For in its talons, limp and still,
There lay an old familiar rag,
Blood seeping past its twisted bill—
A wagtail, then, had been its kill,
And one of a pair no more would wag.

And sure enough, when I woke next day,
I watched its mate dissect the lawn,
Darting in its accustomed way,
But stopping to stare, as if to say,
That even wagtails sometimes mourn.

Early Morning In Dorsington

The cows stand silent in the fields,
Their soft mouths filled with grass and dew.
White mist is rolling down the ridge,
The eggshell sky is milky blue.

Two ducks have landed on the lawn;
My old black cat has caught a doe—
Not badly hurt— I force a thumb
In Moushka's mouth and let it go.

A blackbird struts upon the hedge,
His warbling fit to stir the Bard,
Who, so they say, once walked this way—
(In Warwickshire, old myths die-hard).

The swallows wheel in search of mud,
My bed is made, the dog is fed
And I must down to London town,
Where fools like me must earn their bread.

The Garden Of Life

Our lives are less a journey than a garden
Of virgin soil inherited at birth;
And none but fools would covet, still less pardon,
The motley plants we nourish in its earth;

The bitter fruits of malice and rejection,
The ivy of despair that cloaks a wall,
Tall shrubs of pride, so sure of their perfection,
(Their scabby leaves a wilderness of gall).

And here, a single rose— an act of kindness,
Unsullied by the blight of worldly gain;
But see the nettles, representing blindness
To any other's misery or pain;

And here, the saddest sight— a child's sapling
Stunted in its yearning for the light,
While overhead, dark mistletoe is grappling
With leprous moss as envy succours spite.

And here, a bed of honesty and honour,
(Surprising, is it not, to find it here?
Still, men are all half whore and half Madonna);
This evil copse is nightmare grown to fear.

The sapling? Were it walnut we might whip it,
The ivy will destroy it if it can;
Yet given light, the sapling will outstrip it,
The Tree of Hope was God's last gift to man.

Ghost's Oak

A Kindly Ghost Instructs
His Great-Great-Great-Great-Grandchild

I splashed some water by a well—
It ran into the ground to soak;
Amongst the weed it found a seed
Which grew into a mighty oak.

When famine crept upon the shire,
My grandson stripped its branches bare;
He fed his pigs on mast and twigs
And saved the village from despair.

When war swept down the valley floor,
My great-granddaughter's family
Climbed up amid its boughs and hid
While soldiers razed their granary.

My great-great grandson sold the oak
Which helped to build a galleon
To serve the king, which helped to bring
The downfall of Napoleon.

Her captain was a local lad
Who brought back riches from afar,
His daughter, dear, was raised near here,
And she became your grand-mama.

They broke the ship in seventy-nine,
Dismantling her from mast to hold;
The selfsame wood that once had stood
A mighty oak, was stacked and sold.

Your grandpa bought those beams to build
This very house, and truth to tell,
You sleep tonight upon the site
Where I splashed water— by a well.

Go Not To The Walnut Tree...

Go not to the walnut tree;
Too sober, she,
For such as thee.

Go not to the haughty oak
Who never spoke
To mortal folk.

Go not to the haunted yew
Whose poisoned dew
Would bury you.

Go not to the lusty beech;
She may not teach
Of elven speech.

Go not to the elm, misled;
Her bough will shed
To strike you dead.

Go not to the windy pine;
He makes no sign
To ought of thine.

Go not where the willows flank
The rushy bank;
Their hearts are rank.

Go not to the tall ash tree;
He has no key
To comfort thee.

➤

* * * *

Go to where the rowan grieves,
Go sit beneath the Devil's Bane
In silence, where her trembling leaves
Console the hurts of those in pain.
Last of all her kind, she keeps
Mute memory of human lore:
'Alas! for what is lost,' she weeps;
'Alas! for what can come no more.'

Of all the legends surrounding trees in Britain, those that speak
of the rowan, 'The Devil's Bane', are the strangest. In such myths
and legends, the rowan's power to ward off evil was matched by
an even stranger ability — that of understanding human speech.

Going Bald

My ornamental maples are tenacious;
While oak and alder mourn for what is lost
They sulk in glory, obdurate, ungracious,
Their kamikaze boughs defying frost.

The memory of summer serenades us,
While autumn's fingers tug till we are shorn,
And winter finds us out, and death persuades us
To drop our golden hoard upon the lawn.

The Green Man's Seed

Bewitched within a wood one night
While counting stars by faery light,
I fell asleep beneath a tree,
And there the Green Man spoke to me:

'With counting stars, my mortal friend,
There's little comfort, still less end,
For many now that brightly spark
Have long since winked into the dark.

But since you seek to multiply,
And earth is closer than the sky,
I've planted in your sleepy head
A seed. Think well on what I've said!'

About the woodlands now I go
While counting saplings, row on row.

He has gone by many names over the long centuries, most now forgotten: Jack-in-the-Green, Le Feuillou in France, Blattqesicht in Germany, the Old Man of the Woods, Green George and The Green Man. His enduring attributes are waiting, watching and rebirth. His leaf-wreathed face stares down, usually unseen, from thousands of rafters, walls and bosses in Christian churches of all kinds, Norman chapel and great minster alike. At Exeter Cathedral alone, his image outnumbers that of Christ by five to one. In a saying of the Basque people of present day Spain and France: 'I was here before you came. I shall be here when you have gone.'

The Hornbeams

I walked alone in Golden Square
   One bitter, solitary night,
The littered streets were cold and bare
   With scarce another soul in sight,
The coward lamps flung out their glow,
Chrome yellow on the Soho snow.

St. Stephen's bells began their dance,
   I turned to pace my jaundiced way
To Kingly Street, and then, by chance,
   I felt a snowdrift ricochet
From off my shoulder— raised my eyes
And froze mid-step in mute surprise.

High up above those streets of woe
   Four massive hornbeams clawed the sky,
Each bough a silhouette of snow,
   A sight to paralyse the eye,
To stun the mind and warm the heart
That nature might produce such art.

How long I stood and gazed aloft
   I do not know— then heard a voice
Say 'You alright?' The words were soft
   But coppers leave you little choice:
'Yes thanks,' I said, and met his stare.
He watched me as I crossed the square;

Yet I was musing while I stole
On beauty's power to heal the soul,
And turning back, I chanced to see
A man entranced beneath a tree,
His head bent back, yet strangely bare,
His helmet doffed— as if in prayer.

I Built Myself A House Of Wood...

I built myself a house of wood
Where once an apple orchard stood.
On stormy nights I lay in bed
While rafters moaned above my head.

They wept aloud for limbs long lost,
For buds pinched out by early frost,
For wicker baskets piled with fruit,
For phantom branch and withered root.

I caulked the roof and rafter beams,
But still they whispered in my dreams,
They spoke of rising sap and wood:
And then, at last, I understood.

This spring, I planted out a score
Of apple saplings by my door.
Now stormy nights my rafters chime
To cider choirs and nursery rhyme.

I Have Wasted The Day...

I have wasted the day in the fields and the lanes,
    I have tramped in the leaves and the mud;
I have dined upon air and scrumped me a pear
    And an apple the colour of blood.

Though my fingers are purple from blackberry stains,
    Though my hair is a tangle of straw;
Though my jacket was torn upon bramble and thorn,
    It was worth it for all that I saw.

It was worth all the aches, it was worth all the pains—
    I have rambled and scrambled and raced;
And my stick was mislaid where I dozed in the shade,
And I waded in brooks and neglected my books,
And I startled a hare (and the *taste* of that pear!)
    What waste, what a glorious waste!

Sunday September 29, 2002 was just such a day — an autumnal day when it was good to be alive; when the hedgerows and trees were bursting with fruit, when the sun shone, when the wind was mild, when the leaves on the trees glowed like miniature sunsets, when birds sang and silly squirrels foraged for nuts... the kind of day when only an invalid, a prisoner or an idiot would not have stolen a few hours in what is left of the English countryside. So I did!

I Know A Hidden Field…

I know a hidden field of ridge and furrow
    Far from track or human tread,
Where grasses sigh and coneys burrow,
    Where the cowslips dot the midden,
    Where a skylark hovers, hidden,
       Very high above your head.

I know an ancient road men call The Drover,
    Free of fences, gate or wire;
A chalky way of turf and clover,
    There the hedge is white at May time,
    There a barn owl roosts in daytime
       Snug within a ruined byre.

I know a Druid yew, a silent mourner,
    Mourning what, I do not know.
It stands within a pasture corner,
    Grim with age, grown gaunt and hollow,
    Guarding still some secret sorrow;
       Rot within and grief below.

I know a grassy mound, an orchard parcel
    Tucked beside a hazel wood,
There the lambs play king o' the castle,
    There I've sat amid the cherries,
    Swearing I'd be back for berries—
       Knowing that I never should.

I Looked At A Rook...

I looked at a rook,
He looked at me,
I in my nook,
He in his tree.

He gave such a look
Of scorn and pride,
I shut my book
And crept inside.

I took from a hook
My gun to kill
That haughty rook,
Who meant me ill;

But just as I took
Most careful aim
He gave me a look
That said: '*For shame!*

Before ye came, long, long ago,
These woods were haunt of rook and crow,
Of badger and wolf and doe in flight—
A squirrel could swing from Dale to Bight—
Ye think me rude to thus intrude
Upon thy paltry solitude?
And yet thy gun much ruder is,
For which of us intruder is?'

I looked at the rook,
He looked at me,
I in my nook,
He in his tree;

Back to its hook
Went gun— and, aye,
Back to my nook
Went book and I.

I Plucked All The Cherries...

I plucked all the cherries
Chance would allow,
Take them, and welcome—
I'm done with them now.

Done with the ladder
And done with the tree,
Take them, and welcome—
They're no use to me.

Done with the getting of
What I could get,
Take it, and welcome—
Try not to forget

To pluck all the cherries
Chance will allow,
Take them, and welcome—
I'm done with them now.

In A Soho Garden

Here, in a Soho garden,
Secure from prying eyes,
I lounge in sultan splendour
And watch a spider rise
On threads of silken terror,
Scuttling with its prize
Beneath a fat geranium leaf
To parlours full of flies.

Here, in a Soho garden,
Where blackbirds sing like larks,
Four stories from the alleys
Where foxes shoal like sharks,
I water my geraniums
In floodlit, silver arcs:
Downstairs, the foxes dance on chairs,
While bouncers strip the marks.

I have lived in the same Soho flat in London for forty years now, on the top floor of a court built in the late eighteenth century. My 'rooftop garden' is about the size of a kingsize bed, but it boasts a resident blackbird! And could somebody tell me where all the bees come from in spring and summer? 'Foxes' is cockney slang (rhymes with doxies) for ladies of the night who entice 'marks' (customers) into dodgy nightclubs. I never have seen a real fox in Soho, but other residents claim they have.

Incident In A Sunken Garden

The first I knew was a whirring,
  A birring in the grass,
As if a worm were purring
  In a coat of sea-green glass.

Then I spied a hunter's fury,
  Like Ahab at the mast,
With a spider, judge and jury
  And a dragonfly caught fast.

Four silver wings were thrashing
  To tear its captor's snare;
A bristled maw was gnashing—
  But gnashed upon thin air.

While impulse mocked at duty,
  I plucked him free to fly;
There's little enough of beauty
  To stand and watch it die.

Kestrel

Hover; flicker; flicker; still—
Quartering the empty hill,
Barred wings flare from dart to knife,
Fierce eyes seeking signs of life.

Faultless fury haunts the skies,
Taloned death in beauty's guise,
Banking— drops! and scoops its prey:
Saddened now, I turn away.

The Ministry Cull

By Pasture Brook he waits at break of day
    Beside the wooden bridge, his stick in hand;
The hedgerows, bursting out in wild array,
    Are clothed in white to nurse the injured land.

For silence now is creeping, field by field,
    Across a cankered country, farm by farm,
Where sullen shepherds, swept aside, must yield
    To butchers with their bolt-guns under arm.

They come to cure a plague that cannot kill,
    To serve no earthly good but Mammon's law —
The new-born lambs that gambol on the hill
    Seem not so sick, nor government so poor

That we must warm ourselves at funeral pyres.
    The blood within our veins will scarcely freeze
In early spring, these corpse-filled beacon fires
    Are barbarous cures, far worse than their disease.

The sun has topped the oaks and time grows short.
    His collies bark a warning from the wall;
And yet, their faithless master, sunk in thought,
    Stands idly by while carnage comes to call.

As an owner of thousands of acres of farmland, my feelings over the 2001 outbreak of foot and mouth in Britain were of impotence and rage. Whatever the merits of forcibly slaughtering animals with the disease alongside millions of those still perfectly healthy as a so-called 'precaution', the manner in which it was done was grievously botched. Governmental muddle is one thing; regrettable, but utterly predictable. Far more bitter to farmers and country people was the callous reaction of national newspapers and city-folk. The disconnect between city and country is growing from rift to abyss. There are those, including Government Ministers, who appear to believe this matters not a jot. But they are wrong. So very, very wrong.

Of Flowers We Sing

Of flowers we sing, of bud and shoot,
  Of all that strives toward the light,
Forgetful of the questing root
  Entombed within unyielding night.

Who sings for worm at endless toil?
  For tuber bunkered in the clay?
For blind life inching through the soil
  As poets praise a cherry spray?

The cut bough sickens— soon to die,
  It mourns its anchor in the dark;
Each stately branch that blots the sky
  Is twinned to one bereft of bark.

So saint and sinner share the seed
  Of root and stem, of wrong and right.
Sing as you will, yet each must feed:
  Who sings of light must sing of night.

Of Walls And Fences

Of wrong or right I scorn to sing
(Philosophy pays less than pence),
Instead, I weigh a little thing
Contemptible to common sense—
The rightness of a wall or fence.

If privacy is precious stuff
Then walls exclude a neighbour, true;
Except it puts them in a huff,
And, even worse, it spoils the view—
Such fences need maintaining, too.

Why envy what we cannot see?
Yet cant comes easy to the pen—
Our lives are warped by property,
I've strung barbed wire, and will again.
A wall brings out the worst in men.

Place A Mirror By A Tree

Place a mirror by a tree;
Tell me now, what do you see?

Which of you will feed the earth?
Which of you contains more worth?

Which of you with sheltering arm
Keeps a thousand things from harm?

Which of you is nature's bane?
Which is Abel? Which is Cain?

Which of you is God's delight?
Which of you a parasite?

Place a mirror by a tree;
Tell me now— *what do you see?*

School Outing In A Deserted Hamlet

We stand within an instance of the future
Dry-salvaging the past— note how the moss
Has colonised the crannied bricks and doorframes,
The cankered oak beams twenty feet across;
How grass and bramble pull to their embraces
The shattered tiles and mortar from the floor,
How martins now are nesting in the rafters,
And there, a rusty key still in a door
That once, perhaps, kept children from a pantry,
From bottled jam and cider on the blocks...
Take care! the nettles there conceal old bedsprings,
The cellar now is home to Mrs. Fox.

Wood is strong— but time is stronger,
Bricks and mortar sink to clay;
Iron lives long— but rust lives longer,
Wind and rain sweep all away.

And here, I think, we'll find... the doorstep scraper...
Yes, here, you see, among these bindweed roots,
God help the sons and fathers in a hurry
Who failed to scrape the mud from off their boots!
And here a Belfast sink, now full of spiders
And droppings from a family of mice;
That crumbling work of art was once a mangle,
The cupboard in the corner held the spice.
I shouldn't risk the stairs— the joists are rotten,
The bedrooms house a colony of bats,
The handle here pumped water from the wellhead,
These pegs held Sunday bonnets and best hats.

Wood is strong— but time is stronger,
Bricks and mortar sink to clay;
Iron lives long— but rust lives longer,
Wind and rain sweep all away.

All gone: the whitewashed fence, the byre, the orchard,
The privy, roofless now and soon to fall,
The garden choked with weeds, (save one survivor—
That damask rose you see upon the wall);
All gone, young friends; the wind and rain conspire
To grind away hard centuries of toil,
The beetling years, bedecked with rust and mildew,
Are mindless Goths, in league with famished soil.
We stand within an instance of the future,
Barbarians and levellers at the gate...
You laugh! but mould has little sense of humour:
Earth loves us little— if she knows no hate.

Wood is strong— but time is stronger,
Bricks and mortar sink to clay;
Iron lives long— but rust lives longer,
Wind and rain sweep all away.

Seek-No-Further

[The Walking Apple Tree]

Down the hillsides of New England
Apple blossom scents the air;
Seek-no-further, farmers call them,
English settlers put them there.

Planted them on Dudley Mountain,
Knowing them a tasty bite,
Knowing when an old tree rotted
It must fall one wintry night.

Knowing that its shoots and branches
Walk the hills to spring anew;
Seek-no-further, farmers call them;
If you ate them, you would, too!

I came across the story of *Seek-no-further* apple trees in Eric Sloane's *A Reverence for Wood* published in 1965. According to Mr. Sloane, the first such trees were planted "in the 1700's in Westfield, Massachusetts on top of Dudleytown Mountain" by English settlers. They had brought the seeds from Cornwall. These trees, which have the habit of re-rooting their branches when they collapse, have gradually crept down slopes in many parts of New England, especially Pennsylvania. They are still to be found for sale, sometimes known as Westfields.

Sunset, Mid-July

Sunset, mid-July— the failing light
Salutes a sway-backed cedar on the lawn
And liquefies the words I thought to write:
Not all nights are followed by a dawn,

And not all hurts can ever be put right.
The glory of the world, which sick men mourn
As life leaks out of them, remains as bright
As on the day each living thing was born.

Nor can we stem the tide of coming night—
No man, no cedar, oak or ash or thorn.
Not all hurts can ever be put right,
And not all nights are followed by a dawn.

Sycamore

Some rave of sycamores as if they crept
Upon the countryside, hearts full of vice;
Yet long before this frozen land was swept,
All trees were interlopers to the ice.

A noble sycamore stands even-keeled
And graces many a place with dome and bough;
If she should cast her keys too far afield
What of it, England boasts no wildwood now.

Men manage every inch of these lost lands,
And we have room for beauty; nay, have *need*;
Leave then this mottled wonder where she stands,
And wreak your prejudice upon her seed.

It now seems probable that the sycamore arrived in Britain far earlier than previously thought. They may even have come with the Romans. And yet to hear some 'tree activists' blather on you would believe that *Acer pseudoplatanus* is evil incarnate. I have chased such 'activist's out of my own woods, where they creep about the undergrowth in the hope of wrenching saplings from the earth. The sycamore is a noble tree. It attracts many insects; it is stately in form with multicolored and mottled bark; its boughs are filled with birds and the fast decay of its dropped leaves encourages worm life. It's time to stop playing the 'martyred purist' and welcome sycamores in British streets, fields and woods instead of persecuting and reviling them. We are all 'immigrants' in these isles, after all.

66

Sylva Anathema

From the first flint stroke
    These apes called *folk*
        Have ravaged their hearts' desire;

Our forests awoke
    To grief and smoke
        At the hour they captured fire.

As the seasons turn
    They axe and burn,
        And Weald gives way to plough;

So few of us stand,
    The wounded land
        Lies stripped of root and bough.

I am marked to fell
    But warn them well
        That what they reap, they'll rue;

When their bones are dust...
    Their axes rust...
        We shall cover the earth anew!

Udde-Well Pond

Old Udde-Well Pond is dark and deep,
Its waters shunned by tup and sheep,
The haunt of badger, fox and deer—
Of silent pools and nameless fear.

The black-bricked well is running still
Though none come now to drink their fill;
Udde's odd name carved upon the spout.
White crosses keep the witches out.

For centuries, on muddied tracks,
With yokes and buckets on their backs,
Folk fetched the water, rain or shine,
And left the rest for scaep and kine.

Now, pond and well lie wild, forlorn,
Forgotten, bound in rush and thorn;
I've heard that once, in cruel despair,
A young lass drowned her sorrow there.

Upon The Beach

Upon the beach a solitary tree
   Defies the sea— a shambling stag at bay,
The left side iridescent greenery,
   The right a driftwood copse of salt and spray.

I wade from where the living sap still thrives
   To stroke an antlered bough worn white as bone:
Wet sand sucks at my feet— so time sucks lives,
   The concubine reduced to chaperone.

What lightning strike was this, what storm or wrack
   Wrought ruin in a hydra-headed glance?
Half-naked, with the crab grass at her back,
   She stands, as we must stand, a shrine to chance.

   So ravaged kings on crutches play their part,
   And ghosts of faded beauty stir the heart.

Veteran

What have you seen? Whom did you shade?
How many winters have battered your boughs?
How many seeds did you sow in this glade?
How many beetles and birds did you house?

Where is your crown? Shattered and flayed?
Fear no usurper to topple your throne!
Here you shall stand in your royal glade,
And the day of your falling shall be your own.

Not only does the sight of a battered old veteran conjure the landscape of the past in a way no other living thing can, such trees provide habitat and food for wildlife. Indeed, there are species of lichen and fungi that can live nowhere else. The mania for felling anything and everything in the name of 'Health & Safety', combined with a strange desire lurking in too many human hearts to 'tidy things up', has wrought huge damage to veteran trees in Britain. At the very least, wherever possible, they should be left to their own devices. If a veteran tree on private land should shed a limb and kill anyone foolish enough to to shelter under it during a storm— well, so much the better: there are far too many people in the world in any case. Naturally, a responsible body like The Tree Council could not possibly endorse that last sentiment; but then I am not a responsible body: I am a poet. And poets are 'mad, bad and dangerous to know'. Just like veteran trees!

The Walnut Wood

I want to plant a walnut wood,
To wall it round with Cotswold stone
Without a gate, then quite alone
To sleep until the trees have grown.
I wonder if I ever could?

I want to wake on All-Fools' Night,
Oh, many, many years from now,
To hear the wind through leaf and bough,
To know that neither man nor plough
Has come. To wait for early light,

And walk within my walnut wood,
Both eyes amazed. To choose a tree —
The tallest one! — to speak to me
Of sun and storm and mystery.
Why should all things be understood?

I want to plant a walnut wood.

The Wedding Dress

The woodland trees are decked in reds,
The scarlet blush of newly-weds
Impatient on their wedding night—
Fresh-minted gold their shy delight.

Now jilted summer stands aside
As autumn claims his burning bride,
Arrayed in all her finery,
Displayed for all the world to see.

But honeymoons are short, if sweet,
And time flies by on raptured feet;
Too soon a tyrant's icy stare
Will fall upon fair limbs laid bare.

So I will walk in autumn mist
To see the bride before she's kissed,
Collecting up her leaves to press
A memory— her wedding dress.

The Weeds Of Warwickshire

Their rotting bones lie scattered in each hedge;
I leant on one today and drank some beer,
Attentive to each rough leaf's double edge
While conjuring the shade of what stood here...

Before the beetle plied its lethal trade,
When pestilence rained down in deadly tide
And one by one, those giants on parade,
Succumbed to their peculiar suicide.

Armadas in full sail, fair emerald fleets,
The inshore squadron's glorious men-of-war,
Tall sentinels of shaded village streets,
Of warded pasture, hedge and cottage door.

The Weeds of Warwickshire they called them once,
And shall again as centuries slide by,
These colonies of rotting stools and stumps
Will succour saplings blotting out the sky.

Man's span is short— his tribal lore truncate,
Yet *ulmus minor* flourishes below;
Within the dark, elm's patient roots await
The passing of her parasitic foe.

To tree lovers, the onset of Dutch elm disease was a catastrophe. For elm trees, I suspect, it is a minor irritation, to be endured for a few decades. Elms are alive and well, flourishing even. It's just that we can't see them, except as untidy shoots emerging from felled boles, 'testing the water', so to speak, for parent roots safe in the sanctuary of the soil. So did they commit a form of 'peculiar suicide' to combat this latest invasion? Arboriculturists will swiftly discount the notion as anthropomorphic nonsense. But can it be denied that neither beetle nor pupae nor the disease they carry definitively kill elms? Or that, elms shut down their own sap systems to retreat underground? Just as they have done, we may surmise, in cycle after cycle for millennia.

Whispered The Rowan To The Oak

The woods of our youth are failing,
        even the mightiest rot,
Beetle and high wind take them
        and soon they will be forgot,
Yet sadder than even the fading
        of suns too eager to set
Is that you should fail to remember
        what I can never forget.

The saplings of strangers surround us
        to feather the winter sky,
Yet though you survive beside me,
        you see with an empty eye,
Far better we fall and nourish
        the land in a last duet
Than that you should fail to remember
        what I can never forget.

Whosoever Plants A Tree

Whosoever plants a tree
Winks at immortality.

Woodland cherries, flowers ablaze,
Hold no hint of human praise;

Hazels in a hidden glade
Give no thought to stake or spade;

London planes in Georgian squares
Count no patrons in their prayers;

Seed and sapling seek no cause,
Bark and beetle shun applause;

Leaf and shoot know nought of debt,
Twig and root are dumb— and yet

Choirs of songbirds greet each day
With eulogies, as if to say:

'Whosoever plants a tree
Winks at immortality!'

Why Are You Killing This Tree...

'Why are you killing this tree,
    Wicked old man with a saw?
She has done no harm to thee,
    What are you killing it for?'

'Why this is a hazel tree
    Whose bole has nary a burr;
She has done no harm to me,
    And I do less harm to her.'

'You have chopped it at the knee,
    You wicked old man— you lie!
Why are you killing this tree
    In the woods today? Say why!'

'Though I chopped her at the knee,
    Your Honour may dry his tears,
As a coppiced hazel tree
    She will live a thousand years.'

82

Winter Sunset

All day the snow had lain between the trees,
The barren, hump-backed hills bereft of life,
A sky bruised black, the sleet flung slant to freeze
The bones of man or beast. And then—a knife!

A white-gold knife to blind the sullen gaze
Of Old Man Winter louring in the West;
Three crimson wounds to set the clouds ablaze,
And guide my weary feet to home and rest.

Winter Wood

Beside the gate a cherry stands
In dreamless sleep, her budding hands
Bejewelled with ice and glinting snow—
Pull back the latch and in we go.

The wind has dropped, the light is dim,
An oak has shed a surplus limb
And blocked the ride with branch and bough:
Slip by this birch— tread softly now.

Here's coppiced hazel, lime and thorn,
This wood was old when I was born—
Each twig is father to the tree,
Its replica in symmetry.

A badger's tracks ploughed through the slush,
The creak of heartwood in the hush,
A black crow croaking: 'Get you gone!'
It's home for us; the wood sleeps on.

The Wishing Tree

The Wishing Tree sets thorns and snares,
 Its flashy fruit much bruised,
More tears are shed for answered prayers
 Than ever those refused.

Year's Lease

House Martins in July

Dark silhouettes in search of food
Weave patterns in the sky—
But clumsily. A second brood
Is learning how to fly.

In blurs of metalled blue they dress
And fill the roof with noise;
Beneath each nest, neglected mess—
Like daughters dating boys.

A knife-edged arc across the lawn
Uplifts the heart and eye,
Until that grey, October morn
One meets an empty sky.

You're Bored, Child?

Look at the birds.
Learn to listen to their chatter,
Their flitting, twittering flights for no
Discernible purpose; the clatter
And the cawing of that black crow,
The furtive, dry-leaved peck and scrape
Of blackbirds blundering in a bush
Seeking worms and beetles; the shape
Of the wagtail's wing; the shove and push
Of tits among the bacon rinds;
The eerie, invisible knock,
Knock knock as a woodpecker finds
A bark grub; the wheeling starling flock.

Look at the birds.

Look at the earth.
Scoop up a handful in your palm.
Not for nothing have men plundered,
Murdered, fought and wrought great harm
Among their kind — whole empires sundered —
Just to own it, or to believe
They did. Crumble it. What's it worth?
Ask a farmer stooping to sheave
A field of sun ripe wheat. The Earth!
The land! Listen, listen to me!
The blood of kings lies in your hand,
What came before— and what shall be.
Think on it. Seek to understand.
Look at the earth.

Look at the sky.
An emptiness? The blue-walled womb
Of all that is, of all that ever
Grazed or grew or swam — and met its doom —
Beneath our tyrant sun. Forever
Heaving, blowing, sleeting, snowing,
Raining, resting — bringing with the night
Its velvet, eerie canvas, glowing
With long dead messengers of light.
And yet, who looks— with wit to see?
Should you take long enough to chart
This wheel of time and mystery
Life's miracle will swamp your heart.
Look at the sky.

You're *bored*, child?

A Note on the Poems

The following is in response to questions I am often asked at poetry readings.

I began writing poetry, unexpectedly, in September 1999 while recovering from a life-threatening illness. I was then in my early fifties— pretty late as these things go. One reviewer has observed that I write 'like a man obsessed': perhaps I am subconsciously attempting to make up for lost time? I attempt to write for at least three hours a day on the basis of Mark Twain's dictum that 'most inspiration comes from the application of the seat of the pants to the seat of the chair', and constantly make notes, having discovered that if a promising line or subject arrives in my head, I must reduce it to writing immediately. Delay is often fatal to its recovery.

For the first four or five years I found myself writing four or even five poems a week— a virtual cataract. This has now settled down to two a week or less.

Sometimes I write poetry directly onto my computer. No difference is apparent (to me at least) in the quality of poems created on my computer compared with those begun on paper. When I'm done with a poem, I squirrel it away and try not to refer to it for a year or two, revising only to make selections for a new book or when preparing for a poetry tour. I keep in mind the observation of an earlier poet who said that no poem is ever really 'finished'; merely 'finished *with*' by its author.

Occasionally, I get stuck. Either I cannot write anything worthwhile or I suspect that the form or meter I am wrestling with has usurped the poem's original *raison d'être*. Should this occur, I force myself to abandon the blighter and bang it in a folder marked 'Poems In Progress'. In the early days I tended to soldier on, which often led to second-rate work. Other writers have helped me to come to understand that structure is merely a vessel, not the wine, and that spoiled wine in a fancy decanter is vinegar by any other name. I have also learned that a bad poem, or one merely strong in the weak places, is still a bad poem, no matter what the cost of its birth pains. Some poems arrive effortlessly, others are the result of months of graft. There appears to be (forgive the pun) no rhyme or reason to it.

Audience reaction plays a part in the selection of poems for a new book. While no single audience is infallible, their sustained, collective view is very nearly so, in my experience. Booze helps, but only for up to an hour or so following the first glass of wine; after that, deeply mortifying gibberish is the usual result. Reading the work of other poets is inspirational, but dangerously beguiling. I love to read poetry, but now separate that activity from my own verse-making.

What of intent? Do I write poetry to be performed, to be recorded, or to sit quietly on the page? As anyone familiar with the subject will confirm, some of our finest poets are, or were, poor readers of their own work. (To test this, visit the wonderful website created by Richard Carrington and Andrew Motion, **www.poetryarchive.org** which features, alongside much else, historical recordings by outstanding poets.) Even so, poetry, in essence, is an oral art, a form of song older by far than prose. Rhyme and meter developed partly as a mnemonic device— long before the first hieroglyphs were scratched on rock or bark.

The answer, then, is that I write poetry to be read aloud while knowing that many readers will not follow suit; knowing, too, that only a small percentage will ever attend one of my readings. Instead, my publishers include a free audio CD with my books. Having heard actors from the Royal Shakespeare Company reading my poetry on stage, I am aware that I have neither the talent nor training to match them. Even so, I sit in a studio three or four times a year recording my work. These recordings appear in the audio CDs found in my books, on my own website and others, on the special audio books created by libraries for the blind and, when I'm lucky, on various radio programmes.

Does it all matter? Three years ago a woman came up to me after a poetry reading. She was crying softly. As I signed her book, she kept saying: 'How could you know? How could you know? You are not a mother. How could you know?' She squeezed my shoulder as her husband led her away into the night. So, yes. It bloody well *does* matter— to me and to her, at least.

While it is idle for authors to feign total indifference to applause or brickbats, all in all, I am convinced that I write mainly for myself. I know I would continue to write verse if no other soul in the world expressed interest. I write to discover who I am, to escape the carapace inherited from a life in commerce, to stave off a predilection for other addictions and, primarily, to experience the sheer joy of weaving words to shape ideas. As a somewhat noisome beast, perhaps I should have inflicted my verse-making onto an unsuspecting world anonymously, using a *nom de plume*— the very advice I received from well-meaning friends — but to have done so would have deprived me of the pleasure of performing my work in public.

As Lord Chesterton remarked: 'It is hell to write but heaven to have written.' Amen to that, would say most writers. Why then do we continue to descend into the depths of Chesterton's hell? For some, like Dr. Johnson, the answer might be, 'to make a living': (not that I believe him for a minute). For others, 'to make a reputation' or simply, 'because I can'. For me, it is the result of a chance discovery made ten years ago in a hospital bed: that the flame of poetry cauterises the wound of life as nothing else can.

Any reader wishing to learn more, or wishing to read more of my poetry (published and unpublished) will find a warm welcome on my website at **www.felixdennis.com**

Acknowledgements

Firstly, I wish to thank Pauline Buchanan Black and The Tree Council. The idea for *Tales From The Woods* emerged from my contributions to their splendid magazine *Tree News*. Caroline Rush oversaw each stage of this book's production and Butler, Tanner & Dennis (Britain's finest book printers) will, I know, print it splendidly. George Taylor and Dan Gable recorded and produced the accompanying spoken-word CD with their usual efficiency and creative savvy while Mick Watson's Class Act ensured that my readings are at least technical *tours de force*. Fiona MacIntyre and Carey Smith and their colleagues at Ebury Press somehow continue to sell far more copies of my books of verse than I deserve. On the road, Toby Fisher, Wendy Kasabian, Ashleigh Clarke, Steve Kotok, Catherine Law, Lloyd Warren, Thom Stretton, Julian Guy, Mervyn Hudman and a cast of what sometimes seems like thousands play their heroic parts while, back at the ranch, Ian Leggett, Rebecca Ho, Luke Short, Michael Hyman, David Bliss, Cathy Galt and her team, Don Sheppard and Sharon Islam keep the home fires burning. My editor, Simon Rae, and readers, Moni Mannings and Deborah Boehm, are invaluable— I would be lost without them. Using arcane arts unknown to most mortals, the online staff at Dennis Publishing under Peter Wooton together with Jonathan Noone and Daniel Westall keep my gargantuan poetry website www.felixdennis.com humming. I am especially indebted to the patience of designer Rebecca Jezzard, whose work speaks for itself in these pages, and to Bill Sanderson for his magical illustrations. Thanks, also, to David Tulett and Simon Davies at Point 6 Design for their design input. My thanks are due, too, to the trustees of The Forest of Dennis not already mentioned: Anthony Burton and Julian Dennis. Lastly, as always, I thank the companion of my heart, Marie-France Demolis, together with the many friends I have cheerfully abused as guinea-pigs while auditioning these poems around dining room tables and over countless bottles of wine these past few years.